DIVING AND SNORKELING GUIDE TO

Cozumel
Second Edition

George S. Lewbel and Larry R. Martin

Pisces Books®
A division of Gulf Publishing Company
Houston, Texas

This edition was reviewed by the
authors and reprinted in March 1995.

Library of Congress Cataloging-in-Publication Data

Diving and snorkeling guide to Cozumel / George S. Lewbel,
Larry Martin. — 2nd ed.
    p.   cm.
Includes bibliographical references (p.) and index.
ISBN 1-55992-034-3
1. Scuba diving—Mexico—Cozumel—Guide-books.
2. Skin diving—Mexico—Cozumel—Guide-books.
3. Cozumel (Mexico)—Description and travel—Guide-books.
4. Marine biology—Mexico—Cozumel.
I. Martin, L. R.   II. Title.   III. Title: Cozumel.
GV840.S78L49   1991
797.2'3—dc20   90-25358
                                                        CIP

Publisher's note: At the time of publication of this book, all the information
was determined to be as accurate as possible. However, when you use this
guide, new construction may have changed land reference points, weather
may have altered reef configurations, and some businesses may no longer
be in operation. Your assistance in keeping future editions up-to-date will
be greatly appreciated.

Also, please pay particular attention to the diver rating system in this
book. Know your limits!

Pisces Books®
A division of Gulf Publishing Company
P.O. Box 2608
Houston, Texas 77525-2608

Pisces Books is a registered trademark of Gulf Publishing Company.
Printed in Hong Kong

10   9   8   7   6   5   4   3

Acknowledgments

We wish to say "Gracias!" to the following friends for assistance and encouragement in the production of the first edition of the guide: Pancho Morales (La Ceiba Hotel, Cozumel); Michele Harrison (Poseidon Ventures Tours, Houston); Dick Tompkins (Aqua Safari, Cozumel); Carlos Sierra (Dive Cozumel, Cozumel); Hal Martin (Scuba World, Houston); Karen Young (Underwater Safaris, Houston); Kit Teague; and Sally Sutherland, Kelly Hildreth, and Pancho Contreras.

We are especially grateful to the following friends and fellow divers who assisted in the preparation of this second edition: Bill Horn and Ruth Herrera Hernandez (Aqua Safari); Michele Harrison and Pat Noel (Poseidon Ventures Tours); and Carolyn Martin.

Table of Contents

*Dive sites suitable for snorkeling as well as for diving.

◀ *French grunts, bluestriped grunts, and schoolmaster snappers are often found together resting out of the current. (Photo: L. Martin.)*

How to Use This Guide

This guide is designed primarily to acquaint you with a variety of dive sites and to provide information that you can use to help you decide whether a particular location is appropriate for your abilities and intended dive plan (e.g., macrophotography, high-speed drift, etc.). Hardcore divers who travel fully suited-up with fins, masks, snorkels, and BCs in place on the plane (great for over-water flights with nervous traveling companions!) and expect to leap directly from the plane into the water will find this information detailed on a dive-by-dive basis in Chapter 2.

Read the entire chapter (all dives) before diving, since some material common to several sites is not repeated for each one. Chapter 2, "Diving in Cozumel," and Chapter 4, "Safety," should be read first, however, since they cover both routine and emergency procedures and discuss the system used for rating dive sites for beginners, intermediate divers, and advanced divers. Photographers, fishermen, and budding marine biologists will want to refer to Chapter 3 on marine life, which discusses some of the most common and interesting creatures likely to be seen in Cozumel and summarizes current Mexican fishing regulations that pertain to divers.

Sooner or later, even the most fanatical divers have to come out of the water. Depending on the shore-based facilities, this can be a cause for rejoicing or weeping. As you know, there is an illustrated brochure for virtually every Caribbean diving destination showing the usual beach scenery, palm trees, divers on boats, lobsters on platters, and so on. Perhaps you have been to other locations that offered fine diving but that could have been improved by scraping off everything above the waterline and starting over. This most assuredly is *not* true for Cozumel. Although the diving in Cozumel is spectacular, taking the time to let your gear dry will give you an opportunity to enjoy one of the most charming islands in the Caribbean. Chapter 1, "Overview of Cozumel," offers a brief description of the island's history, geography, scenery, natural history, and some general information on accommodations, services other than diving, shopping, and other useful tips.

Lush growth and sheer dropoffs typify Cozumel's reefs. These formations, such as Palancar and Santa Rosa, are justifiably famous. Since the mid-1950s, thousands of divers from all over the world have marveled at this island's underwater wonders. (Photo: L. Martin.) ▶

The Rating System for Divers and Dives

Our suggestions as to the minimum level of expertise required for any given dive should be taken in a conservative sense, keeping in mind the old adage about there being old divers and bold divers but few old bold divers. We consider a *novice* to be someone in decent physical condition, who has recently completed a basic certification diving course, or a certified diver who has not been diving recently or who has no experience in similar waters. We consider an *intermediate* to be a certified diver in excellent physical condition who has been diving actively for at least a year following a basic course, and who has been diving recently in similar waters. We consider an *advanced* diver to be someone who has completed an advanced certification diving course, has been diving recently in similar waters, and is in excellent physical condition.

You will have to decide if you are capable of making any particular dive, depending on your level of training, recency of experience, and physical condition, as well as water conditions at the site. Remember that water conditions can change at any time, even during a dive. The rating system we've used is shown schematically in a chart in Chapter 2, "Diving in Cozumel."

Nestled under the protective arm of Mexico's Yucatan peninsula, Cozumel provides some of the most spectacular diving in the hemisphere.

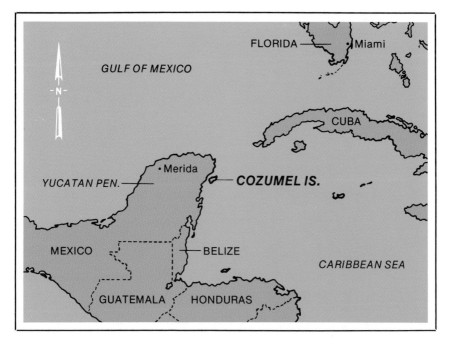

1

Overview of Cozumel

Cozumel Island is located near the eastern tip of the Yucatan Peninsula in the Mexican State of Quintana Roo. The island is about 30 miles (48 kilometers) long and about 10 miles (16 kilometers) wide. Due to its proximity to the mainland, the center of Mayan culture, the island was under Mayan influence for many centuries. Even today many residents of Cozumel show a striking resemblance to carved and painted images of pre-Columbian Mayans, and many locals still speak a Mayan dialect as well as Spanish. Some Mayan ruins may be found in the jungles on the island, although the most famous and spectacular archaeological sites are on the mainland (e.g., Chichen Itza, Cobah, and Tulum). These sites can be visited on one-day tours leaving from Cozumel; reservations for tours can be made at almost any hotel or at the airport.

The island has long been a favored spot for travelers. In pre-Conquest times it was a religious center for Mayans, and subsequently it was visited by such notables as Hernán Cortez (who conquered Mexico for Spain during the sixteenth century) and a number of pirates who took advantage of the abundant fresh water on the island and the calm, deep waters near the western shore to anchor and rest between raids. More recently, the island has been invaded by thousands of divers seeking clear, warm water. Today Cozumel has a most unusual blend of cultures, successfully integrating divers (nearly all American) with the resort industry of modern Mexico and the local Mayan heritage.

◀ *Blue chromis graze a constant source of planktonic food brought by the prevailing current off Cozumel. (Photo: L. Martin.)*

Natural History

Both Cozumel and the peninsula are low-lying terraces of limestone covered with jungle. The limestone is derived largely from coral that has been solidified and compressed into hard rock over the eons. You can see the fossilized imprints of shells and corals from ancient reefs that make up the limestone if you look at it carefully along the shore. Much of the coast of Cozumel (especially along the western side) has no sandy beaches but rather is made up of eroded limestone or "ironshore." On the eastern side, sandy beaches cover the ironshore in many areas. The limestone is porous, retaining rainwater like a sponge and slowly dissolving. As a result, a halo of fresh water is sometimes seen in the ocean near some spots on the coast. The jungle is dotted with fresh-water springs, caverns, wells, and pools *(cenotes)*, which may contain brackish or fresh water depending on the level of the water table and the amount of seawater that can intrude through passageways in the rock. At the southern tip of the island, salt marshes create a swampy environment that attracts and holds tourists' vehicles like a magnet.

The island is separated from the mainland by a channel only 12 miles (19 kilometers) wide. On most nights, if you look to the west, you can see a few lights of the Yucatan coast from the shores of Cozumel. Most of the mainland coast looks pitch dark at night, however, since most of Yucatan is still solid jungle (yes, the real kind with hanging vines, poisonous snakes, and parrots and monkeys in the treetops); the only clearings are an occasional ranch or farm and the *cenotes*. For that matter, nearly all of Cozumel Island is jungle, too. If you go hiking, look out for snakes and don't sit on fire ant hills. Fire ants are small, ordinary-looking insects that are to other ants as chile peppers are to tomatoes.

Weather: Due to the rather constant temperature of the water currents that sweep around the island, the climate on Cozumel is predictable although not entirely stable. The annual average air temperature is about 80°F (27°C), and you can expect temperatures in the high 80's to low 90's°F (about 32°C) in July and August, and in the mid-70's F (about 24°C) in December and January. Water temperatures range from about 77°–82°F (25°–28°C). However, December and January can see cold fronts from the Continent that can create windy, cloudy, and cold weather. A cooling breeze usually blows day and night. Afternoon thundershowers are common but seldom last more than an hour. Fall sometimes brings hurricanes to the Caribbean, but their paths usually bypass Cozumel to the east.

◄ *Lush gorgonians populate shallow sandy areas where rocky substrate is available for attachment. (Photo: L. Martin.)*

Cozumel Island Today

About a third of the western-facing shore of Cozumel has been developed into a dense strip of modern hotels along a single road that runs within a few hundred feet of the beach. The strip is separated by the road from the jungle. Taxis patrol this strip day and night, dueling with brave tourists on mopeds.

The hotel row runs north and south from San Miguel, the only town on the island. San Miguel is a typical small Mexican town in some respects, with tiny shops, narrow streets, and a pretty central plaza. In the last few years, however, San Miguel has had to come to grips with its international position as the main service center for an island besieged with divers year round. By and large, it has made the adjustment gracefully. There are many small, inexpensive hotels in town within walking distance of the plaza, restaurants ranging from very inexpensive to fairly expensive, several department stores and markets, liquor stores, a number of dive shops (look for the red and white divers' flag everywhere), car and moped rental agencies, and the ever-present Mexican curio and handicraft shops.

The larger hotels outside town have their own shops and restaurants, and it's possible to spend your entire vacation without venturing into town if you stay in one of the beachfront resorts. You'll be missing a good bet, though, if you don't go into town at least one evening to shop and look around.

The hotel row south of town is popular with divers because of the available dive sites just off the beach. (Photo: L. Martin.)

Cozumel's International Pier hosts an ever-increasing stream of cruise ships, ferry boats to the mainland, and other commercial vessels. For your own safety, don't dive or swim near the pier. (Photo: L. Martin.)

Hotels

Virtually all of the hotels on the island cater to divers. They can be divided fairly easily into two general categories: luxury (resort) hotels and simpler, less expensive hotels. Several condominiums have recently been completed. They tend toward luxury.

The luxury hotels are located along the waterfront to the north and south of town. They generally have every amenity that one would expect in an international facility, including swimming pools, air-conditioned rooms, restaurants, gift shops, and the like. Many of the luxury hotels have dive shops on the premises, and most of them have easy entries and exits (such as concrete steps) at the waterline so that you can go diving right in front of them. Several hotels that have particularly good diving from their own beaches or piers are mentioned in Chapter 2.

The simpler hotels are located in town within several blocks of the plaza. Some are air-conditioned, some have restaurants in them (but are within easy walking distance of dozens of other restaurants), and all are much less expensive than the luxury hotels. The simpler hotels usually do not have dive shops on the premises, but nearly all have some working arrangement with one or more dive shops so that you can arrange equipment rental and boat diving through them. Most of the simpler hotels are located near the center of town, within walking distance of dive shops.

Because all of the reefs mentioned in this book are south of town, and because nearly all dive operators run boats to the south every day, hotels to the north of town are decidedly less desirable for divers. The boat rides are longer the farther north you go, and many operators will not pick you up north of town. That means worrying about missing the boat in the morning, and salty, wet taxi rides at the end of the day.

There are a few problems that seem to crop up again and again for divers on Cozumel. Most of these problems are related to lodging. Making reservations in Mexico has always been a bit tricky, but it is more so than ever at this time. Since the peso has been declining in value with respect to the U.S. dollar, the occasional holiday rush has been replaced with a steady onslaught of American divers wanting to take advantage of low Mexican prices and a favorable exchange rate. At the same time, hotels and diving facilities that purchase supplies and equipment from the States have been caught in a bind; their pesos buy fewer dollars, and Mexico has been suffering from an inflation rate averaging well over 50% a year for most goods.

As a result of all the confusion, it is extremely important for the hotels to have every room occupied if at all possible since they are making less money per person. A number of Cozumel's hotels have responded to this pressure by "overbooking," that is, selling more rooms than they have available.

At this time, therefore, we must recommend against counting on individual reservations with hotels on Cozumel unless you have paid for the rooms in advance, have written receipts with you from the hotel showing dates of arrival and departure and amount paid, and are sufficiently familiar with the hotel that you know they will honor your reservation. We also recommend that all correspondence by mail with Mexico be sent Registered, especially if bearing checks or other items of value.

Tipping

Tipping in Mexico is similar to tipping in the U.S. The range for excellent service is 10–15%, and the trades relying on tips are those traditional ones that cater to travelers (waiters and waitresses, cab drivers, hotel staff, dive guides, etc.). Be sure to check your hotel or restaurant bill to see if service is included *(servicio incluido)* in the charges; if it is, no tip is expected.

Transportation

Car Rentals: Rental cars can be arranged by almost every hotel or condominium, but it is not uncommon to have every car on the island reserved. The best procedure is to reserve a rental car through an international company that is represented in the States. Most of the larger companies have an office at the airport; some also have offices at the luxury hotels. Driving is on the right-hand side of the road, Mexican style, with the likely possibility of arrest and detention in case of an accident, so be on the defensive and be sure to buy insurance. If you're feeling brave, the larger hotels and a number of highly visible shops in town (within a block of the plaza) rent mopeds. You'll recognize them by their huge signs and the fleets of motor bikes parked in front. See the section on Documents at the end of this chapter for further information on car rentals.

Taxis: While you can rent a car to get you to shore diving locations or to shops, taxis are abundant and very inexpensive, and you may find it convenient to leave the transportation to them. The cost of a taxi ride is fixed within town and along the hotel strip, and the prices posted in each cab. If you want to go around to the eastern side of the island, though, renting a car is preferable; you'll want to stop to have a beach all to yourself, and you almost certainly won't be able to summon a cab to pick you up later. There are virtually no phones outside of town and the hotel strip, so before you go adventuring tell someone where you're going, and make sure you can change a flat tire!

Foreign Exchange, Dining, and Shopping

Foreign Exchange: Nearly all of the hotels, stores, and restaurants on the island are used to dealing with foreigners. In addition to the divers from the U.S.A., several cruise liners dock at Cozumel every week, disgorging hundreds of tourists. Consequently, U.S. dollars are accepted nearly everywhere at very close to the official exchange rate. Our experience has been that it's not really worth the trouble to try to get a few cents more by standing in line to exchange dollars at the bank unless you're really a high roller. Currency other than U.S. dollars or pesos may present problems, however, and a bank visit may be required. You can buy pesos at many banks and airports in the States as well as in Mexico in case you want to get this out of the way in advance.

The local economy is heavily dependent on divers and other tourists. The handcrafted products found in shops or from individual craftsmen, such as this hammock maker, make excellent buys.
(Photo: L. Martin.)

Dining: Even if your Spanish is rusty (or nonexistent) you'll have no problem getting what you need on the island. Most restaurants have menus in English and Spanish, and almost every restaurant, store, and hotel has someone on staff or within reach who speaks English. Cozumel may be the easiest place in Mexico to visit if you don't speak Spanish, although any attempts to communicate in Spanish (even high-school Spanish!) will be graciously received and encouraged.

Restaurant dining therefore will present no unusual challenges to visiting divers. Seafood is the island specialty, and frech conch, lobster, and fish are served proudly by most restaurants. Though temperatures remain warm all year, the dress style all over the island is diver-elegant (i.e., t-shirts or light sports clothes), and you won't need to take your tie or dinner jacket anywhere.

Shopping: With regard to shopping, most consumer goods such as canned or packaged food at markets are imported from the United States.

Consequently, don't expect any bargains on American products whatever the peso/dollar exchange rate may be. These goods are purchased with dollars and shipped from the States into Mexico (picking up some taxes along the way). Gourmands note: the shops are used to catering to post-dive muchies fits, and most food stores sell Danish cookies, fancy Dutch and Swiss chocolate bars, and similar vital commodities. Make sure they aren't melted before leaving the store. We once had a heartbreaking experience on a sunny day with a pile of vital, emergency-use-only, raspberry-filled bittersweet candy bars . . .

There are many Mexican souvenir items available, and the best buys may be had on these. As in other Mexican locations, high-quality sterling silver jewelry, handmade blankets, hammocks, serapes, carved onyx chess sets and figurines, and simulated pre-Columbian pottery are sold by most shops. *Caveat emptor* is the rule of thumb, although the stamp "sterling" on silver can almost always be relied on as its use is controlled by the Mexican government. Expect to bargain for souvenir-type items, with the original asking price perhaps double the final selling price, but don't bother haggling in any of the department stores or markets selling imported

---

La Turista: Avoiding and Treating It

Perhaps a word of advice on sanitation might be welcome here, given the cost of a diving vacation and the unhappiness of having to sit out a dive due to illness. Throughout most tropical countries (Mexico included), it's a good practice not to consume any water or ice cubes that have not been purified (ask for *agua purificado* or carbonated mineral water, *agua mineral con gaz*). You will also increase your chances of avoiding difficulties if you don't eat salads or uncooked vegetables, peel all fruit, and take a prescription antibiotic just in case.

If worse comes to worst and you catch Montezuma's revenge, there is a pharmacy *(farmacia)* within the large market-department store at the northeast corner of the plaza, and the pharmacy will generally dispense whatever you need, even drugs that are available only on prescription in the States, if you know what to ask for and how to use it. The paranoid diver (ourselves included) has his own doctor set up a medical kit before leaving home, taking into account the possibility of catching the *turista* on the road. Kaopectate® or Pepto-Bismol® works for mild cases, while Lomotil® (prescription required in the U.S.) is your serious "cork-in-a-jar"!

goods. Lots of souvenirs seem to be designed mainly for divers, such as carvings of sea creatures and turtle-shell combs, rings, and bracelets. Sea turtles are on the Endangered Species List for the U.S., however, and it is highly illegal to import any turtle-shell items into the States. Customs will seize them (and you, if you try to sneak them in) upon your return.

Documents

A word to the wise about documentation and international travel is included here. To get into Mexico you'll need some proof of citizenship (e.g., passport, birth certificate, voter's registration). If you're bringing along any minors who are not accompanied by *both* parents, you must have a notarized, detailed letter from the absent parent or parents giving you permission to take the child into Mexico for a vacation.

On your arrival in Mexico, you'll be issued a Mexican Tourist Permit — a thin blue-and-pink document complete with signatures and rubber stamps. Don't lose it! You'll need the Permit to leave Mexico, and may be asked to show it at any time by Mexican officials. When you leave Mexico, you'll turn in your Tourist Permit along with a departure tax ($10 U.S. as of this time, but subject to increase) if you fly out.

Driver's License: If you plan to rent a car or moped, you'll need your U.S. Driver's License, as well as a major credit card or a giant wad of cash to show you can financially cover any damage to the vehicle.

C-Card: Unless you have your diver's certification with you, you will not be able to rent tanks or charter boats. In other words, no card, no diving, no fun.

◄ *The ruins of San Gervasio near the center of the island provide an attraction on those rare days when the sea is too rough or when divers just want some surface time. (Photo: L. Martin.)*

2

Diving in Cozumel

This book describes a number of popular spots and some that are less frequently dived but well worth seeing. Several shore dives are listed, and you will find that a few fine days can be spent diving from the shore for the cost of a taxi ride or two to entry and exit areas. Some reefs can be dived either from boat or shore, depending on how energetic (or lazy) you feel. Other reefs are best dived by boat.

The branch of the Gulf Stream that sweeps along the north/south-oriented island produces currents that range from barely perceptible to well over three knots. The farther offshore one goes, the stronger the current (usually). The finest diving may be found on the crest of a near-vertical wall that runs the length of the western shore of the island. Since this shore faces the mainland across a narrow channel, the weather there is usually much better for diving than on the eastern shore.

While there are spots on the eastern shore that can be dived during some conditions (e.g., strong west wind), these are not described in this guide because of the difficulty of access and the typically marginal water states.

This book includes comments on typical depths and current conditions and the level of expertise required to dive each site under ideal conditions. You should keep in mind that most of the reefs mentioned are very large, and this dive guide has been compiled to give an overview of what to expect. Consequently, it is possible to find deeper (or shallower) areas than those mentioned as typical of each site, and currents may be much stronger or weaker than anticipated on some days. Shoreline entry and exit spots can change with time, too. Your best source of information about any location will probably be local divers, especially those working for charter dive operators or shops, since they are familiar with the range of possibilities at each site.

Spectacular colors and shapes such as this brittle star and red sponge are common in Cozumel. (Photo: L. Martin.) ▶

Some Useful Techniques

Because typical conditions on the western side are calm seas but strong currents, drift diving is the norm for boat diving in most locations, especially those on the wall. As in any open-water situation, you should always carry an emergency signal device such as a whistle, and, if far from shore, an additional device capable of being seen from far away, such as a flashing strobe or inflatable signal tube.

For boat dives, a "live boat" technique is generally used by charter boat captains, who follow divers' bubbles to greet them at the end of the dive. A dive guide is often provided at both ends of a group of divers in order to keep them together while on the reef and to aid pickup at the surface. Be sure to describe your previous experience, swimming abilities, and any special concerns to the divemaster or dive guides on the boat. Given the strong currents around Cozumel, we do not recommend that you rent a boat on your own without a local dive guide and captain. There are special skills required to operate a "live" boat safely around divers, and Cozumel's waters favor using professional operators only.

For shore dives, an exit spot some distance down-current must be selected (and inspected) in advance, since it may be impossible to return to the starting point up-current. Booties and gloves are recommended to deal with ironshore. Many hotel piers can serve as excellent starting and end spots for shore dives. They often feature ideal entrances and exits, such as concrete steps and ladders, and are generally placed in areas sheltered from strong currents. Transportation can be found easily at both the start and end of a dive at hotels. Taxis sometimes park at hotels, waiting for business, and the hotels can always call a taxi for you while you're dripping dry! Don't worry about carrying money with you to cover cabfare at the end of a dive; cabs will wait while you run inside your hotel to get your money.

If you are planning to dive from the shore, be sure not to swim any farther than your capabilities allow for a safe, easy return, and ask the local divers to help you to evaluate water conditions before jumping in. You should also take along a dive flag on a float. The usual current direction is parallel to shore from south to north, with speed increasing as you get farther offshore, but the current sometimes reverses direction and occasionally can take a seaward course. Before your dive, arrange with someone on shore to keep watch along the expected drift pathway and to meet you at your exit point at a given time. That way, if you have any problems en route, help can be summoned promptly.

The information above should suggest that Cozumel may be enjoyed by divers with a wide range of skill levels. For wall dives in particular, an experienced guide will add considerably to your safety and comfort. The charter dive operators do not, at present, always separate experts

Sponges grow under a ledge on the downcurrent side of a coral head. (Photo: L. Martin.)

Many hotel piers make excellent entrance and exit points for shore dives. Be sure to plan your dive carefully so you know exactly where the exit will be and watch for boats when near or on the surface. (Photo: L. Martin.)

from novices on boat dives. For a beginner, to be dropped over a vertical wall in a strong current may be an exciting situation to say the least. Even for the pro there are a few surprises possible. For example, when high-velocity water runs into a coral buttress, zones of rapid upwelling and downwelling develop. Being caught in one of the down-slope currents is similar to being flushed in a gigantic toilet, and divers must be aware of their depths and surroundings at all times.

A little specialized practice on buoyancy control, drift-diving techniques, and deep-diving methods with a qualified instructor can go a very long way toward ensuring a pleasant, safe trip. This instruction should be arranged with the dive shop or charter operator before getting on the boat, however, as dive guides may have their hands full and not be able to offer any instruction without prior appointments. Furthermore, the majority of dive guides on the island are just that — guides — and are not diving instructors. Again, set up any instruction you may need in advance.

We consider diving on or near the lip of sheer walls to be safe only for advanced divers and for intermediate divers, and then only when accompanied by a qualified diving instructor or divemaster. Novices should never place themselves in any situation where loss of buoyancy control can result in rapid depth increases. This translates as advice to keep away from the edges of walls, dropoffs, or buttresses. When high-velocity currents are present, even more caution is indicated. We have rated most *drift* dives, except those very near shore (e.g., Paraiso South), as appropriate only for advanced divers and for those intermediates diving with an instructor or divemaster. We have rated some boat dives as appropriate for novices, but only when diving with an instructor or divemaster.

The typical two-dive boat trip includes a lunch break at one of the popular beaches, thus extending the surface interval between dives. (Photo: L. Martin.)

Typical Dive Operations

Dive operators on Cozumel Island vary considerably with respect to their punctuality, the purity of their compressed air, the reliability of their boats, and — most important — their concern for your safety. Some operators employ well-trained guides who are also diving instructors, while others may only hire local divers familiar with reef locations. Some boats carry first-aid kits, some carry oxygen, some have radios, and others don't. Some use tanks that are new, while others use tanks that may not have been hydrostatically tested for fifteen years. Rental gear ranges from "donate-it-to-the-Smithsonian" vintage to near-new, depending on the operator.

At this time, the diving industry on Cozumel is expanding rapidly, and represents a vital economic resource to the island. Your business is anxiously sought by dive operators for this trip and for the next. You do have the right — and, perhaps, the responsibility — to demand first-class service from dive operators in exchange for your money. In the spirit of better, safer diving, we urge you to ask questions about those matters you consider important to you as a diver, and to reward only those operators you are satisfied with by giving your business to them. You can have a positive influence on the future of diving on Cozumel and at the same time increase your safety and enjoyment. For example, we tip a boat dive guide only if he treats our group courteously, provides a complete pre-dive briefing on the site and safety procedures, and keeps a watchful eye on the group in the water. No one likes to think about diving accidents, but consider, just for a moment, how an injury to you or your buddy would be handled, and don't be satisfied with vague answers.

Dive Boat: There are many dive boat operators on the island. Three types of boats are commonly used: 1) open "flat-tops," with broad decks that offer easy suiting up and entries and exits; 2) traditional diesel-powered modified fishing boats (motor sailers) that ride very well in rough weather but tend to be slower than other types of boats; and 3) modern, high-powered runabouts and small cabin cruisers that are fast and stable even in rough seas. You may enjoy the roominess of the flat-tops, or prefer the relaxed pace of the motor sailers, or instead just want to get to and from the dive site as fast as possible. You can make the choice if you ask the operators what kind of boats they run before booking trips. Rather than book all your diving with one operator, you might consider sampling several shops to see how they compare to one another. As we mentioned, there are lots of differences.

Most of the operators offer two-tank trips, providing tanks, backpacks, and weights, with lunch included between dives. The lunch usually is

Cozumel dive boats have evolved to modern, faster vessels, increasing comfort and safety for divers. (Photo: L. Martin.)

served on San Francisco Beach, a beautiful white sand strip heavily patronized by local Mexican families as well as visiting divers. The most frequently visited part of San Francisco Beach has bathrooms, restaurants and bars, live music, and good fun. Alternatively, some operators prefer a more remote section of the beach where charcoal-barbecued fish and isolation are the attractions.

Shore Diving: If you are diving from the shore, you will find it extremely easy to rent tanks, backpacks, and weights at the many dive shops in town, at the hotels, and at the well-known Chankanab Lagoon. Most shops rent aluminum cylinders. Older cylinders holding 70 cubic feet at 3000 psi are presently more common than newer 3000 psi 80's, so look carefully before you rent. Hot, short fills unfortunately are pretty common on Cozumel, although less likely to occur at the larger shops. It's worth the trouble to gauge your rental tank before carrying it away from the shop. If you want to go diving after 5 P.M., plan ahead — most shops close about then.

Dive Site Ratings

	Novice Diver	Novice Diver with Instructor or Divemaster	Intermediate Diver	Intermediate Diver with Instructor or Divemaster	Advanced Diver	Advanced Diver with Instructor or Divemaster
1 Paraiso Reef North			x	x	x	x
2 Airplane Flats*	x	x	x	x	x	x
3 Paraiso Reef South*		x	x	x	x	x
4 Chankanab*	x	x	x	x	x	x
5 Beachcomber Cavern					xC	xC
6 Tormentos			x	x	x	x
7 Yocab			x	x	x	x
8 El Paso del Cedral			x	x	x	x
9 Tunich					x	x
10 Cardona		x	x	x	x	x
11 San Francisco				x	x	x
12 Santa Rosa				x	x	x
13 Palancar				x	x	x
14 Punta Sur					xD	xD
15 Colombia				x	x	x
16 Maracaibo					xD	xD
17 Colombia Shallows*	x	x	x	x	x	x
Sand Diver's Secret	x	x	x	x	x	x

Rating system:

x = Dive is appropriate for a given level of expertise under favorable water conditions. See Chapter 2, "Diving in Cozumel," and descriptions of individual dive sites (following in this chapter) for further information.

* = Good snorkeling spot.

C = Specialized training in cavern and cave-diving techniques required before making this dive.

D = Specialized training in deep-diving techniques required before making this dive.

When using this chart, refer to the previous section entitled "The Rating System for Divers and Dives."

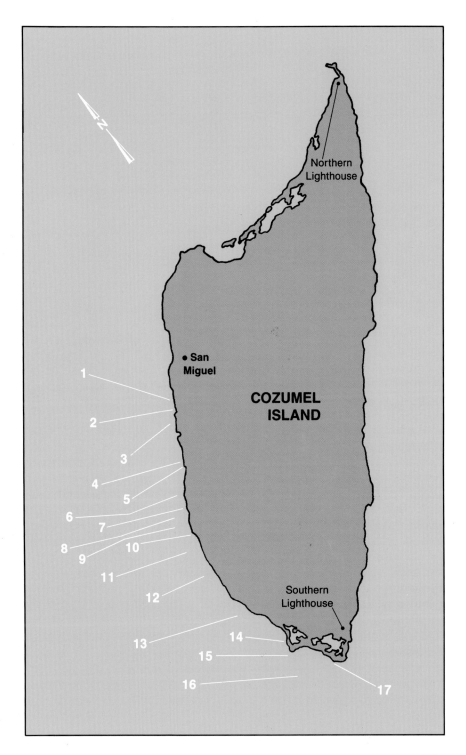

Northern
Lighthouse

COZUMEL
ISLAND

● San
Miguel

1

2

3

4

5

6

7

8

9

10

11

12

13

14

15

16

17

Southern
Lighthouse

Typical Depth Range:	40–50 feet (12–15 meters)
Typical Current Conditions:	Light to moderate, occasionally strong
Expertise Required:	Intermediate
Access:	Concrete steps at La Ceiba Hotel or via the small beach cove at Sol Caribe Hotel

Paraiso (Paradise) Reef North is a series of backbone-like strips of coral running parallel to the shore. The series can be intersected by swimming perpendicular to the shore out to a depth of about 40–50 feet (12–14 meters). If you exceed this depth you've missed the reef and gone too far, and you should turn around and head back toward shore. Paraiso Reef North lies just seaward of the sand flat that is marked at its shoreward edge by the sunken airplane (see the description of Airplane Flats). To find Paraiso North, swim from the plane straight offshore toward the wall, bearing slightly to the right (northward). It is about a five-minute swim from the plane.

The reef consists of large coral heads and sponges up to 6 feet (2 meters) in diameter. Large schools of iridescent blue chromis fishes form

Bar jacks are often seen over sand near slopes and dropoffs. (Photo: L. Martin.)

◀ *These large knobby coral polyps are cavernous star coral. They come in a variety of colors and are a principal reef builder. (Photo: L. Martin.)*

On days when the current is light, you can have a wonderful, relaxed closeup look at many of the smaller organisms just offshore the La Ceiba and Sol Caribe hotels. (Photo: L. Martin.)

clouds above the reef, and if you hunt carefully around the sandy bases of the big coral heads you may catch a glimpse of the blue-, white-, and yellow-striped splendid toadfish. Paraiso North is not large — a few hundred feet long — and is probably best visited as part of a longer dive, perhaps starting at this reef and proceeding inward to end near the airplane.

Paraiso North is far enough offshore to be subject to the influence of strong currents, and if you're headed to or from this reef you may have to correct for drift. If you're carried northward by the current you will find the handiest exit at the Sol Caribe pier. If you're carried southward, stay on the bottom, avoid the area of the International Pier, and exit at the La Ceiba Hotel. There is often boat traffic between Paraiso North, the Sol Caribe, and the La Ceiba, so if you're on or near the surface you should keep alert and be prepared to get out of the way of vessels that may not see or avoid you.

Airplane Flats* 2

Typical Depth Range: 10–35 feet (3–10 meters)
Typical Current Conditions: Light
Expertise Required: Novice
Access: Concrete steps (several sets) along the water between La Ceiba Hotel and Dive Cozumel's dock, or via the small beach cove at the Sol Caribe Hotel

Airplane Flats is an area that stretches from in front of La Ceiba Hotel on the south to just north of the Sol Caribe Hotel. Most of the terrain is rather flat, but there's lots to see. Snorkelers will find this an excellent spot to see fish and gorgonians (sea fans). There is also wreckage of an old airplane that makes a dramatic backdrop for photographs. Snorkelers can rent gear from the full-service dive stores at most of the hotels along the waterfront.

The Mexican federal government made the western shore of Cozumel a national marine park to help protect the many unusual species found here, such as the splendid Cozumel toadfish. (Photo: G. Lewbel.)

Placed here as a prop for a movie by film director Ramon Bravo more than 13 years ago, this sunken twin-engine airplane was saved for divers by the owner of the La Ceiba Hotel. Storms and time have taken their toll, but the wreckage provides excellent habitat for all kinds of marine life. (Photo: G. Lewbel.)

Due to easy access and lights at the hotels and docks, this is a near-perfect site for night diving. If there's any current running, you might consider jumping in at the up-current end of the site (usually, but not always, La Ceiba) and exiting at the down-current site (usually Dive Cozumel or the Sol Caribe) to save yourself some swimming.

In any event, don't dive or swim south of the La Ceiba Hotel, and stay well clear of International Pier. The International Pier is illegal to approach closely due to the hazards presented by cruise liners, ferry boats, and other vessels. For that matter, quite a few boats pick up and drop off divers at the various piers bordering Airplane Flats. Keep your eyes open on the surface, and don't ascend without checking for approaching traffic. The hand you save could be your own!

Near shore, there are some elkhorn coral heads, though the best formations were battered by a major hurricane during 1988. Long-spined sea urchins are common around these coral heads and near shore. Be careful not to touch them or step on them! Beds of gorgonians begin at a depth of around 10 feet (3 meters) and continue seaward on a shallow shelf. Most of the gorgonians are on the shallow shelf near shore. The shelf is ideal for snorkelers. At night, basket stars are frequently seen spread out on top of gorgonians, feeding in the dark. There are also big open areas on the shelf with a few small coral heads. These areas are excellent places to look for large rainbow parrotfishes, especially when the sun is low in the late afternoon. You'll see them feeding on the bottom, picking at plants and chunks of coral. The shallows are patrolled by territorial damselfishes that despite their diminutive size are inclined to nip at offending divers.

The shelf breaks at the edge of a sand flat about 30 to 40 feet (9 to 13 meters) deep, where a low-profile coral reef replaces the gorgonian beds a few hundred feet from shore. The most characteristic species are leaf or ribbon corals. This reef is an ideal first dive for training purposes, or a good warmup dive for novices and rusty veterans. There is enough open space over the sand to practice buoyancy control, and there is enough fish action to keep the dive interesting. The coral is not in very good shape due to heavy traffic and storm damage, but you'll find plenty of things to see. The fish are accustomed to handouts, so don't be surprised if you're mobbed by Bermuda chub or sergeant majors.

A patch of red encrusting sponge is growing over this mountainous star coral. (Photo: G. Lewbel.)

North of the airplane along the shallow limits of the sand flats lie the remains of an old boat, which several species of fish call home. (Photo: L. Martin.)

If you follow the edge of the break in slope to the north in front of the Sol Caribe and the Dive Cozumel/Divers' Inn complex, you'll find the ribs of an old wooden boat at a depth of about 30 feet. The boat is a hang-out for big schools of grunts, snappers, and the occasional grouper. It's a great spot for fish photography. You may also be lucky enough to see the largest sand tilefish in Cozumel; his nest is just north of the boat ribs.

A bit farther out, there are the remains of an old twin-engine prop plane. At this time, it lies on sandy bottom directly out from La Ceiba Hotel in about 40 feet (12 meters) of water. Storms have moved it around a bit, and will continue to do so, but it usually is marked with a surface buoy by the hotels because it's such a popular dive site. Be careful not to get snagged in any lines, and look out for sharp edges. The airplane has been very good for Band-aid sales on the island. Many fish have made it their home. Its surface remains fairly clean due to the scraping bites of parrotfish, whose toothmarks can be seen on the metal along with the graffiti of thoughtless divers. Also, look for purple patches of sergeant major eggs on the plane. They'll be guarded by expectant — and aggressive — parents.

Typical Depth Range:	35–45 feet (11–14 meters)
Typical Current Conditions:	Moderate
Expertise Required:	Novice (with qualified instructor or divemaster)
Access:	From the second telephone pole (#56) on the shore just north of the yacht basin *(caleta)* on the north side of the El Presidente Hotel, or via boat

Paraiso (Paradise) Reef South consists of two long ridges of coral running parallel to shore end-to-end, at depths of about 35–45 feet (11–12 meters), surrounded by sand. It is frequently visited by charter boats as a second dive after a deeper wall dive. It is also a favorite among dive operators for night dives, since it is a short boat ride from most hotels, and is fairly shallow. It may also be reached easily from the shore. It's a bit deep for most skin divers, but the nearshore ridge is a good reef to snorkel over and watch scuba divers. Look out for boat traffic!

Clubbed anemones are common on the reefs surrounding Cozumel. (Photo: G. Lewbel.)

Red and orange sponges splash the sides of a coral head with their brilliant color. (Photo: L. Martin.)

Paraiso Reef South is home to many tame fish that have been fed by dive guides. If you're hoping to see large, bizarre filefish, or French and gray angels within arms' reach, you'll probably not be disappointed. The coral formations are medium-sized and this entire reef is relatively low in profile. The small crevices at the bases of the coral heads shelter many squirrelfish during the daytime, and serve as "toeholds" for the six-foot-long (2 meters) sea cucumbers that stretch out on the sand at night to feed. The reef is ideal for photographers, since depth control on the fairly level bottom is far simpler than on any of the walls. If you're planning to make a wall dive during your stay on Cozumel, you'll find that when the current is running Paraiso South is a good place to get some experience in drift diving techniques over level bottom before you hit the dropoffs.

We recommend this as a beach dive only when there is no current. Most of the reef stretches to the north of pole #56. The easiest access to this dive is to leave your car (if you have one) at La Ceiba Hotel, and take a taxi around the *caleta* just north of the El Presidente Hotel. The road will pass the harbor and then return to the coast. Get out at the second telephone pole (#56), walk into the water (sand and a few rocks), and swim straight offshore over sand and seagrass until you intersect the reef (about 5–10 minutes' swim). The first major dark streak out from shore is seagrass; the second is the reef.

If you're diving from a boat and planning a drift dive, your options are greater. If the current is running to the north, drift along the coral ridge with it. The first ridge is several hundred yards long, and ends abruptly at its northernmost point in sand. If your air and bottom time permit, continue swimming toward the north, but angle to your left (westward or seaward) about 30° when you leave the first ridge. You will come to the southern tip of the second ridge within a minute or two. The second section parallels the shore, but slightly seaward of the first, and is about the same in length. The second section also ends in sand at its northern tip. If the current is running to the south, ask to be dropped on the northern tip of the northern ridge, and do the dive just described in reverse.

Tame fish such as this French grunt are a photographer's delight at Paraiso Reef South. (Photo: L. Martin.)

Chankanab* 4

Typical Depth Range:	10–35 feet (nearshore coral heads) (3–11 meters)
Typical Current Conditions:	Light
Expertise Required:	Novice; good snorkeling and skin diving location
Access:	Walk into the water down concrete steps

Chankanab ("Chankanaab" on some maps) is one of the most popular shore dives on the island. This site is ideal for training purposes and for "rusty" divers to refresh their skills before diving the deeper sites. There's a beautiful botanical garden here, too.

Chankanab boasts facilities for gear rental and air fills, and is a popular weekend location for island residents due to new picnic facilities and shops selling snacks. It's also one of the more common sites for moped crashes due to the large, economy-sized speed bumps installed in the road, so be careful!

Concrete steps and ladders provide extremely easy access to the ocean. The bottom immediately adjacent is about 10 feet (3 meters) deep. There are large schools of tame fish — especially grunts and snappers — that can nearly always be found under large ledges within a few yards of the steps. Photographers will find these fish cooperative and very used to divers, since they've appeared on several posters.

The area just offshore has tall patch reefs separated by sand channels. The bases of the coral heads are especially good spots to find spotted drums and jacknife fishes. Local tourist interests have placed a small wrecked fishing boat on the bottom just a few hundred feet off the steps (look for the mast sticking out of the water), and an assortment of old cannons and anchors on the sand flats near shore. All in all, this dive must be considered one of the best on the island for beginners in terms of easy access, diversity of marine life, and convenient facilities.

A squirrelfish lurks beneath a sponge-covered outcrop. (Photo: L. Martin.) ▶

Typical Depth Range:	10–35 feet (3–11 meters)
Typical Current Conditions:	Access and cavern entrance, light to none; inner portion, unknown
Expertise Required:	Outer cavern, advanced with specialized training in cavern or cave diving; inner portion (cave), not recommended
Access:	Steps at Chankanab, or by boat

Just to the south of the main entrances/exits at Chankanab are several entrances to a large cavern that lead to a cave which penetrates the island for an unknown distance. The site is often called Beachcomber Cavern in memory of a fine seafood restaurant (the Beachcomber) which used to sit above the entrances. The restaurant has since been removed, but the site can be found easily without this landmark.

To get to the entrances, swim on the surface a few hundred feet south (parallel to shore) from Chankanab, staying close to shore until you are facing a large channel-like cut in the shore. Face the shore and you will see a narrow boat channel about 20 feet (6 meters) wide and about 10–15 feet (3–5 meters) deep. It's open on the seaward side and comes to an abrupt end about 50 feet (15 meters) in from the shoreline. You'll be

---

Hazards

Divers are cautioned that specialized training and equipment for cavern or cave diving techniques are essential to enter the cavern or cave safely. If you do not have this training and equipment, stay outside the entrances. If you bring a flashlight to the entrances, you will be able to see nearly all of the outer cavern without having to go inside yourself.

The cave has not yet been mapped, although a few local divers have penetrated it for some distance. Due to lack of information about the inner portion, the authors must recommend strongly against entering any sections of the cave except for the outer cavern, that is, the area in which divers can remain within sight of and immediate reach (one breath) of an exit to the outside. Diving the inner portion should be only by experts equipped and trained for exploratory cave diving.

A mass of silver fingerlings boils out of the entrance to Beachcomber Cavern. While inside, the small nooks and crannies protect them from larger predators. (Photo: L. Martin.)

looking at the mouth of it from the seaward side. There has been some move to reconstruct a building next to the channel, so by the time you read this there may be a structure on the left of the boat channel. The main entrance (and exit) to the cavern is just to the left of the cut, on the north side of the rocks that mark the northern edge of the cut. The main entrance is shaped like an inverted triangle, about 10–15 feet (3–5 meters) on a side. There are several alternative entrances and exits on the north side of the boat channel. Most of these openings are large enough for several divers to pass through side-by-side, but if there are any waves or swells you should stay out of the channel to avoid getting beaten around by sloshing water.

The main entrance to the outer cavern is usually filled with small, silvery fish that form a solid-looking curtain from surface to bottom and from side to side. The curtain will part dramatically as you swim through.

Both the main and alternative entrances open into the outer cavern. The outer cavern consists of a large central room about 20–30 feet (6–10 meters) in diameter and about 10 feet (3 meters) high, supported by numerous pillars. The outer cavern ceiling does not enclose any airspaces, but has some small holes (too small for a diver to fit through) that allow beams of sunlight to get through in spots. Several dark, smaller side rooms open onto this central room, and tunnels lead to the inner portion of the cave. The outer cavern and the inner cave have areas of soft, silty bottom that can be resuspended in the water by swimming, so be very careful not to stir up the bottom or you'll lose your visibility! Within the dark cavern you'll be able to see a variety of nocturnal fish (glassy sweepers, bigeyes, glasseye snappers) and possibly a large grouper or two taking a nap during the day. A few urchins sometimes hide near the entrances in the shadows, so use your lights before touching down.

Fungus coral grows best at the bases of coral heads.
(Photo: G. Lewbel.)

Glassy sweepers hover just inside the mouth of Beachcomber Cavern. With their oversized eyes, these hachet-shaped fish prefer the semi-darkness of the cave to the dazzling brilliance of the daytime reef. (Photo: L. Martin.)

The Green Mirror

This cavern is famous for a peculiar hydrologic phenomenon that can result in some amazing photographs. Fresh water has saturated the island and, in some locations such as this, seeps back into the sea as if from a sponge. The fresh water is usually colder than the ocean, but it is so much less dense than salt water that it floats on top if protected from turbulence. The cavern provides this protection, allowing a *reverse thermocline* with warmer water below colder water. The fresh water usually forms a brilliant green-colored band a few feet thick on the surface. Sometimes it even produces a mirror-like reflective layer three or four feet (one meter) beneath the surface. Try to see it on your way in before your bubbles and turbulence have disturbed the layer. It's most visible from within the cavern, looking outward through the entrances. After you leave the outer cavern exits you can feel the cold, fresh water on the surface, and see the shimmering mixing layer where the salt and fresh water combine.

Tormentos Reef 6

Typical Depth Range:	50–70 feet (15–20 meters)
Typical Current Conditions:	Strong
Expertise Required:	Intermediate
Access:	Boat

This reef is similar in many respects to Yocab and El Paso del Cedral reefs. The coral heads on Tormentos Reef are a bit taller (10 feet) than those on Yocab, and a bit lower than those on El Paso del Cedral, but the fauna and topography are comparable. The back sides of the coral heads provide resting places out of the strong south-to-north prevailing current, and you'll find endless subjects for macrophotography on the undersides of the heads. Lobsters and nurse sharks are also abundant in the crevices on the north sides of the coral heads. Tormentos is a great place to see big black groupers, smaller yellowmouth or scamp groupers, barracudas, and pairs of white-spotted filefishes.

Tormentos Reef is long enough so that you're likely to burn a full tank before you run out of coral onto the sand. If you lift off the bottom into the current, you'll usually be carried along at a knot or two without putting any effort into swimming. To take a break, just duck behind a coral head and hug the sand on the downstream side. For your safety stay with your fellow divers (especially your dive buddy) and your dive guide.

Large old sponges are prevalent at high current sites. (Photo: L. Martin.) ▶

Divers and fish alike take refuge behind coral formations from the prevailing current at Tormentos. (Photo: L. Martin.)

Typical Depth Range:	50–70 feet (15–20 meters)
Typical Current Conditions:	Moderate to strong
Expertise Required:	Intermediate
Access:	Boat

Yocab (also spelled "Yucab" on some maps) is sometimes dived as a second dive of the day on boats, as it is possible to see a good deal of the reef without exceeding 50 feet (15 meters). Yocab is strongly recommended to those who like the reef running parallel to the current direction (north/south) and surrounded by brilliant white sand bearing large ripple marks that can be attributed to the strong current that usually sweeps over the area from south to north. Large coral heads stick out of the sand to a height of 5–10 feet (2–3 meters); on the down-current sides of these heads divers will find some refuge from the current and a truly marvelous collection of animals also hiding out in the backwaters. The down-current northern ends of coral heads have been sculptured and weathered by sand scour, and many caves and ledges there harbor schools of fish, large

Smooth trunkfish and an abundance of other reef creatures are found hiding from the prevailing current in the undercuts of Yocab Reef. The current generally runs from south to north, and the northern sides of the large coral mounds are marked by scoured-out tunnels, arches, and caves. (Photo: L. Martin.)

Coral heads on Yocab Reef extend up 5–10 feet (2–3 meters) above the sand bottom, which is about 50 feet deep. Many of the heads exhibit a dazzling array of colorful growth, with several varieties of sponges, corals, and gorgonians sharing a single boulder. (Photo: L. Martin.)

lobsters, crabs, and the like. Photographers probably will be frustrated by the current in most spots, but may shoot down "on the deck" in the eaves of the coral heads. Fish will be seen drifting along with divers on days when the current is strong! Very large white-spotted and scrawled filefish frequent Yocab Reef.

Yocab Reef comes to a distinct northern end, marked by a huge coral mound at about 60 feet (18 meters). Beyond this mound the sand slopes rapidly downward toward the wall, and divers will want to make their ascents on sighting this mound at the tip of the reef. As with other drift dives, it is important to stay together with your guides or divemasters, since charter boats usually drift above groups, following their bubbles and picking up all divers together at the end of the dive.

Typical Depth Range:	40–60 feet (12–18 meters)
Typical Current Conditions:	Strong
Expertise Required:	Intermediate
Access:	Boat

El Paso del Cedral Reef is a long, backbone-style reef similar to Yocab and Tormentos. All three reefs have large, relatively low-profile coral heads along a ridge that separates a shallow sand flat from a deeper sand flat. The terrain on El Paso del Cedral is higher in profile than at the other two reefs, but there are more sandy stretches between coral heads at El Paso del Cedral. The tops of the coral heads lie in the 40–50-foot depth range, with bases in sand on the seaward side at closer to 60 feet. Most of the coral heads are in a fairly straight line with respect to prevailing currents, meaning that you can ride the flow and see most of the reef. After you think you've run out of coral, a gentle left turn across the sand will take you over an additional section of coral.

This reef boasts very large schools of porkfish, French grunts, cottonwick, and snappers that rest out of the current in small caverns and notches on the north, down-current side of the coral heads. As at Tormentos and Yocab, it's very important to stay with your buddy, your group, and your dive guides. If you slip out of the current and everyone else is still drifting with it, they'll blow downstream out of sight in a few seconds, and vice versa.

Schools of grunts, such as these bluestriped grunts, and snapper are commonly scene at El Paso del Cedral. (Photo: G. Lewbel.)

The higher profile of this shallow reef forms caverns, which are not present at reefs of similar depths, such as Yocab and Tormentos. (Photo: L. Martin.)

Typical Depth Range:	60 feet (18 meters) minimum to unlimited (dropoff)
Typical Current Conditions:	Strong
Expertise Required:	Advanced
Access:	Boat

Tunich lies along the edge of Punta Tunich, between Punta Tormentos and San Francisco Beach. Tunich is almost always washed by strong currents. Expect an exciting, high-velocity drift dive along the rim of a dropoff. The currents are usually strongest near the rim. Unlike many of the more traditional reef dives on Cozumel, Tunich does not have steep buttress and groove coral formations. A beautiful white sand flat at about 60–80 feet borders a fairly gentle slope that falls off at around 45° toward

French angelfish are easily spotted on the open slope at Tunich. (Photo: L. Martin.)

The scenery along the dropoff at Tunich is dominated by huge sponges. (Photo: L. Martin.)

the abyss. The edge of the dropoff is an excellent place to see schools of bar jacks and larger pelagics such as turtles and eagle rays, though their appearance is not predictable, of course. Thousands of other fish are usually there, including huge rainbow parrots and groupers, and more queen triggerfish than you're likely to see anywhere else.

The main attraction at Tunich is the huge basket sponges. Why do all their cavities face toward the north, away from the current? A basket sponge draws water in through its outside surface, extracts oxygen and nutrients from the water, adds carbon dioxide and wastes, and dumps the filtered water out the central cavity. The cavity faces down-current so that water that has already been filtered can be carried away, and the current at Tunich nearly always runs toward the north. Other kinds of low-profile sponges are also common at Tunich. Look for big, flat brown patches up to 10 feet across, with small siphons sticking up to pump exhaled water away. These flat sponges, in particular, should not be touched; they can produce instant "sponge rash" and itching.

Typical Depth Range:	20–45 feet (6–14 meters)
Typical Current Conditions:	Light
Expertise Required:	Novice (with qualified instructor or divemaster)
Access:	Boat

Cardona Reef is located a short distance north of San Francisco Reef, too far offshore for a beach dive. It is a good choice for a second boat dive, since most boat operators stop for lunch at nearby San Francisco Beach after visiting Palancar, Santa Rosa, or Colombia. It's a very worthwhile spot, too, if you've already had enough parrotfishes and giant coral heads for the time being. Cardona might be considered a connoisseur's reef, mainly interesting to divers looking for unusual species of fish. Bring a flashlight on this dive. Cardona is a low-profile reef that has relatively few big coral heads, but instead is better known for its long ledges and overhangs. Most of these ledges parallel the shoreline, forming a series of ridges.

Barred cardinalfish hide among the miniature spires of a colony of pillar coral at Cardona Reef. The striped spines of a long-spine urchin, another hiding place favored by the elusive cardinalfish, can be seen at the lower right. (Photo: G. Lewbel.)

The undersides of many of the ledges at Cardona Reef are covered with green algae. Nocturnal fish, such as squirrelfish and glassy sweepers, often hide in the dark recesses beneath these ledges during the day. (Photo: G. Lewbel.)

If you're used to diving in cold water where there are a lot of algae and you've been wondering where the plants are on coral reefs, look under these ledges. You'll find bright green, wingnut-shaped algae hanging down in areas of reduced light.

Nocturnal Fishes by Day

The ledges at Cardona Reef provide shelter for some very large schools of nocturnal fish that hide under the overhangs. As a general rule, you can recognize nocturnal fish by two characteristics: first, they're hiding in caves and other dark places during the daytime; and second, they have big eyes with large pupils for effective night vision. Look for the hatchet-shaped glassy sweepers, the red-and-silver-barred glasseye snappers, and a variety of squirrelfishes. Cardinalfishes are also easy to find at Cardona, though they often hide among the spines of sea urchins. If you're taking pictures, you'll probably be able to get close enough to these small, beautiful fishes for a good strobe-lit shot, since many of the ledges are very large and roomy enough to lie beneath.

Typical Depth Range:	20–60 feet (6–18 meters), but near a wall (depth unlimited)
Typical Current Conditions:	Moderate to strong
Expertise Required:	Intermediate (with qualified instructor or divemaster)
Access:	Boat

San Francisco Reef is located directly offshore from San Francisco Beach. It consists of a fairly low-profile coral strip on the lip of a dropoff. If you have never made a wall drift dive, San Francisco Reef might be a good one to start with, since the edge of the dropoff is shallower than many of the other walls on Cozumel. In some places, the lip is as shallow as 20 feet (6 meters), though 50–60 feet (15–18 meters) is more typical. Even if you have lots of experience on walls, you'll really enjoy the extra bottom time you can get on this reef by staying shallow.

The reef is an excellent spot to see filefish, angelfish, trumpet fish, and other common reef species. It is also known for its tentacle-faced *(Stoichactis)* anemones, which look like beds of small green grapes up to a foot across. The many nooks and crannies on San Francisco Reef shelter large lobsters, and you can often find bigeye, sweepers, and other nocturnal fish hiding in the crevices during the daytime. If you stray off the reef and over to the west, you'll be looking down into the dropoff; the white sand to the east is a good place for stingrays and conch.

Coneys come in various colors. This red one lurks behind coral as divers approach. (Photo: G. Lewbel.)

A dive light will reveal spectacular colors beneath the overhangs. (Photo: L. Martin.)

Typical Depth Range:	50 feet (15 meters) minimum to unlimited (wall)
Typical Current Conditions:	Moderate to strong
Expertise Required:	Intermediate (with qualified instructor or divemaster)
Access:	Boat

Santa Rosa Reef shares a number of features with Palancar, Colombia, and the other coral buttress areas on the lip of the dropoff. It has tall columns of coral with vertical walls cut by channels which slope from the white sand bottom on their shoreward side down near-vertical, terraced

Santa Rosa Reef, like Palancar and Colombia, is a series of coral escarpments on the edge of a vertical wall. As at the other walls, the current here is typically strong. Divers should stay close to their group and carefully monitor their own time and depth, because others may be diving a different profile along the deep dropoff. (Photo: L. Martin.)

The wall at Santa Rosa is riddled with caves, grottos, and tunnels that are among the best on the island. The insides of these are often home to spectacular filter feeders — vase, tube, and rope sponges, and giant sea fans. (Photo: L. Martin.)

canyons on their seaward side. As on the other buttress reefs, enormous plate corals, mammoth-sized sea fans, and spectacular sponges are common at Santa Rosa. The best diving is along the seaward faces of the buttresses, where divers can look down into blue depths and up along sheer cliff sides. Santa Rosa does differ from the other reefs in the diversity and quality of its caverns and grottos, though. If you want photographs or views of divers silhouetted in the mouths of caves or dropping through narrow slots between walls, this is your reef. Tame, hand-fed groupers are common here, too. Lately, several small blacktip sharks have frequented Santa Rosa.

Santa Rosa Reef is known for strong currents, so drift diving is the norm. Be sure to monitor your own depth and time, because other divers may follow different dive profiles up and down the walls. Stay together with your dive guides or divemasters and with your group, as "live" boating is typical and you will all be picked up (ideally in a group) down-current from your starting spot.

Typical Depth Range:	40 feet (12 meters) minimum to unlimited (wall)
Typical Current Conditions:	Moderate to strong
Expertise Required:	Intermediate (with qualified instructor or divemaster)
Access:	Boat

Palancar Reef, the most famous on the island, is renowned for its towering coral buttresses. Similar in topography to Colombia Reef, Palancar is a long stretch of apartment-house-sized columns reaching as shallow as 30–40 feet (10–12 meters) in some areas but anchored on the edge of a vertical dropoff. Between the columns are white sand channels and caves on the sheer sides of the buttresses. It is possible to stay shallow at Palancar by not descending between buttresses or along the seaward faces, but most of the diving is along the outer wall.

Perhaps the most famous of all Cozumel reefs is Palancar. Towering columns of coral line the edge of a sheer wall that drops from 40 feet at the tops of the columns into more than a hundred fathoms (more than 600 feet). (Photo: G. Lewbel.)

Brilliant sponges are common along the tops of the coral ramparts that line the dropoff at Palancar. (Photo: G. Lewbel.)

An especially popular area of Palancar, called the Horseshoe *(la Herradura),* has been the subject of many photographic studies and posters. Another excellent area for a second dive is Palancar Gardens, which has miniature buttresses, canyons, and terraces, with dropoffs starting as shallow as 30 feet (10 meters). It is not possible to "see Palancar" in one dive or twenty, since the reef is tremendous in size, and charter operators frequently visit different areas of Palancar to provide variety for their clients. If you take pot luck, you won't be disappointed.

Strong currents are common in the area, and most boats operate unanchored, dropping divers off upstream of the dive site and picking them up at the other end. Stay together with your group and with your guides or divemasters to facilitate pickup once on the surface, and, as with any other wall dive, be sure to monitor your depth and time carefully, since other divers in your group may not dive the same profile you choose due to the "bottomless" nature of the vertical walls.

Typical Depth Range:	100 feet (30 meters) to unlimited (wall)
Typical Current Conditions:	Strong
Expertise Required:	Advanced with specialized training in deep-diving techniques
Access:	Boat

Punta Sur lies near the southern end of Cozumel, and is deeper than most other wall dives on the island. Along the crest of the dropoff, there are large buttress formations of coral with caverns and channels similar to those at Santa Rosa. The tops of the formations reach 60 feet or so at the shallowest, but most of the good scenery lies below 80 feet on the

Huge towering buttresses with large caverns are typical of Punta Sur. (Photo: L. Martin.)

Divers should watch their depth and exercise good buoyancy control at Punta Sur. (Photo: L. Martin.)

face of the wall. The bases of the buttresses grade steeply into a sandy slope at depths too great for sport diving. The inshore sides of the buttresses rest on a deep sand flat (120–130 feet). Much of Punta Sur looks like a single long row of apartment buildings rising sharply on both seaward and inshore sides. The inshore sand flat spills over between the buttresses and flows down the dropoff, producing beautiful sand "waterfalls" and rivers.

This dive site is rapidly developing a reputation as one of the best places to find pelagic fishes such as sharks, horse-eye jacks, and eagle rays. Too deep for most divers, its coral and sponges have not yet felt the impact of careless knees and misplaced fins. With any luck, it will remain the province of very experienced divers, who (presumably) will have the necessary buoyancy control and diving skills to keep it in pristine condition.

Typical Depth Range:	60 feet (18 meters) minimum to unlimited (wall)
Typical Current Conditions:	Moderate to strong
Expertise Required:	Intermediate (with qualified instructor or divemaster)
Access:	Boat

Colombia Reef is one of the great coral buttress areas located along the lip of the dropoff toward the southern end of the island. Huge pillars of coral loom over white sand on the shoreward side and slope downward on the seaward side to successive terraces below them. The tops of the pillars are mostly in the 60–70 foot (18–20 meter) range, while the narrow passageways and channels between them open onto the nearly vertical faces of the seaward side. You will find gigantic plate corals and huge sponges interspersed with anemones, gorgonian sea fans, and a wide

Colombia Reef is a continuation of the towering coral buttresses that characterize the reefs on the south end of the island. The coral formations are interspersed with broad sand channels. (Photo: L. Martin.)

Large gorgonians line the wall near the lip of the dropoff at Colombia Reef. (Photo: G. Lewbel.)

variety of other attached organisms. Many fish live among the pillars and in the holes, caves, and crevices formed by the reef. Photographers will probably want to set up for wide-angle work, at least on a first dive, as the three-dimensional relief of Colombia Reef is second to none in the world.

The typical boat dive on Colombia Reef will be a drift dive, since strong currents are common here. Some protection from water movement can be had on the back side of pillars and in channels, but divers can expect to cover quite a distance on one tank. As on all other wall dives, your selection of depth can range from the tops of the pillars to whatever your own judgment (and your guide) will permit. Your boat will probably operate unanchored, picking up your group at the end of the dive, so be sure to stay together with your dive guides or divemasters and the rest of your group. It's a long way to shore! Current direction on Colombia is quite variable, and large eddies and swirls are typical.

Typical Depth Range:	100 feet (30 meters) to unlimited (wall)
Typical Current Conditions:	Strong
Expertise Required:	Advanced, with specialized training in deep-diving techniques
Access:	Boat

Maracaibo Reef is a deep reef at the southern tip of the island. If you want to dive Maracaibo, you'll probably have to get together with enough people to charter a boat and captain for the day (rather than ride on an "open" boat). In general, the captains on the slower boats will refuse to dive Maracaibo, since the run there and back takes a full day. The boat trip is not only longer than to the other major reefs, but also deeper. All members of your party should be advanced, very experienced divers trained in deep-diving techniques. Due to its location, Maracaibo is less protected from weather and the ride there is often wet and rough, so if you're prone to seasickness you might sit this one out.

Maracaibo is a buttress reef, with the inshore edges of most buttresses at depths of 100 feet (30 meters) or more. The offshore wall lip is at least 120 feet (36 meters) deep in some locations, so watch your depth gauge! The coral formations of Maracaibo resemble the other large dropoff wall reefs (e.g., Palancar, Santa Rosa, Colombia), with tunnels and caves and vertical walls interspersed with broad sand channels. Very large buttresses are typical of Maracaibo. It's not worth the trouble to get to Maracaibo just to see coral, however. You can see spectacular coral and sponges at the other reefs more easily, less expensively, and with a shorter boat ride.

Shark Watching, Maybe!

Many of the divers that go to Maracaibo go to see sharks. Sharks are frequently spotted at Maracaibo, but (just like that noise in your car that disappears when you take it to the mechanic) you can't count on them. Blacktips (several closely related species) are most common, but it is possible to encounter hammerheads, shortfin makos, lemons, tigers, or bulls. Keep in mind, though, that you pay your money and you take your chances. Some years few sharks are seen, and other years sharks are seen on most dives. Big schools of eagle rays and mantas have also been seen at Maracaibo.

Pay particular attention to your depth gauge when descending on Maracaibo because you may be surprised how quickly you approach your depth limit. (Photo: L. Martin.) ▶

Typical Depth Range: 20–40 feet (6–12 meters)
Typical Current Conditions: Light
Expertise Required: Novice
Access: Boat

Colombia Shallows is inshore of Colombia Reef. A convenient two-tank day of diving would start on the wall at Colombia and move in to the Shallows for a second dive. However, Colombia Shallows is rarely visited because most boat operators prefer to take divers to Paraiso, Yocab, or other more northerly reefs (near lunch and home port) on their second

Colombia Shallows is made of huge vertical coral formations that rise toward the surface from a sand bottom at about 40 feet. (Photo: L. Martin.)

Colombia Shallows exhibits much more vertical relief than the other shallow Cozumel dive sites. (Photo: L. Martin.)

dive of the day. Some of the charter boats don't carry two tanks per diver, and stop at San Francisco Beach between dives to change tanks and have lunch. These boats almost certainly will not turn around and run south to Colombia Shallows after lunch, so if you want to dive these southerly reefs back-to-back, be sure to make the necessary arrangements before leaving the dock.

Colombia Shallows is a good area for beginners, since currents tend to be light and there's lots of clear space to sit down on sand and between walls of coral. It's a great place to practice hovering. It's like a miniature Palancar Reef without hordes of other divers. Furthermore, the restricted bottom depth lets photographers take wall-type shots without fear of dropping off into an abyss while focusing. Snorkeling is excellent above the coral heads, but look out for boat traffic!

Sand Diver's Secret

Typical Depth Range: Wherever you find sand flats
Typical Current Conditions: The full spectrum, from none to strong
Expertise Required: As indicated for the nearest other dive listed
Access: Boat or shore

If you enjoy diving away from the crowds, and need a change of scene, Sand Diver's Secret is for you. You won't find it on the map, but you already know how to get there — just stop on the way to or from your favorite reef, or take a detour away from the dropoff out onto the sand. Chances are good that your fellow divers will think you've lost your way. You can surprise them when you bring back a detailed log and a roll of film of all the things you saw on the sand that they didn't see. Most of the diving on Cozumel takes place over reefs, which account for a very small fraction of the actual diveable area. There is a lot more sand than

A diver discovers a heart urchin in the sand flats. (Photo: L. Martin.)

This school of smooth trunkfish is hunting by jetting water from their mouths to uncover food hidden in the sand. (Photo: G. Lewbel.)

coral. Divers who get dropped over sand flats usually keep their heads up and their fins moving until they find "the dive site" (i.e., the coral). They thereby miss some of the most interesting animals and one of the most fascinating habitats underwater. That's the Sand Diver's Secret.

To appreciate the sand flats properly, you'll have to get right down on the deck with your mask a few inches from the sand. Notice that the sediment differs in coarseness from one sand flat to another, and within a sand flat from spot to spot. The smallest particles collect where current velocities are lowest, and vice versa. Water movement can easily carry off fine particles, whereas coarse, gravelly sand requires faster currents to move it. The texture of the sand provides an index of the average current velocity. Big chunks indicate high speeds. Fine, soft sand means low current velocity.

Many inhabitants of sand flats, such as this electric ray, lack the brilliant colors of reef fish and are better able to blend into the background. (Photo: G. Lewbel.)

The patterns of marks in the sand can also tell you something about water movement and direction. High-speed currents heap coarse particles into big sand waves, while slower currents produce only ripple marks in finer sand. Larger sand particles are found toward the tops of the sand waves or ripples, and finer particles collect in the quieter water in the troughs between the waves. Ripples and sand waves are oriented 90° to the average direction of water movement, just like sea fans, and can therefore be used to help you navigate on the bottom.

Many so-called "infaunal" animals live in sandy environments, including clams, burrowing shrimps and other crustaceans, and worms. Most of them are large enough to see, but remain buried below the surface where they are invisible to divers. Deeper burrowers have tubes leading to the surface so that they can get food and oxygen, and discharge wastes. Infauna sometimes filter plankton from the water, or feed on microscopic "meiofauna," tiny animals that live between the sand grains, forever wandering in a maze of particles that must seem as huge as boulders to them.

"Epibenthic" animals live on or near the surface of the sand, sometimes feeding on infauna or other small attached plants. Some epibenthic animals are tiny, such as the schools of clear mysid crustaceans (the size of brine shrimp) that usually are mistaken for juvenile fishes. Larger forms include heart urchins, hermit crabs, and conchs, which can be found by following their tracks across the sand. Heart urchin tracks look like meandering ridges a couple of inches high. Conchs leave a smooth groove. Hermit crab tracks show small depressions where their legs touch the bottom and an irregular trough where the shell drags. Sea stars, long-spined urchins, and big snails such as tritons are also prominent epibenthic beasts. Because other animals eat them too, quite a few epibenthic species are nocturnal, spending the daytime buried in the sand or beneath the edges of coral heads.

A variety of predatory fishes feed on infaunal and epibenthic animals. Rays, peacock flounders, guitarfishes, and skates treat the sand flats as

The ability of this peacock flounder to alter its coloration aids in avoiding detection on a variety of bottom colors. (Photo: G. Lewbel.)

a cafeteria with an excellent selection, open 24 hours a day. Sting rays dig obvious pits in the sand by flapping their "wings" and excavating worms and clams. These pits are sometimes six feet across and several feet deep. Other fishes such as bar jacks and smooth trunkfishes hover above feeding rays, picking out any stray infaunal animals that are stirred up by the rays. If rays aren't working, trunkfishes can do their own smaller excavations by blowing water out of their mouths onto the sand. You can attract both bar jacks and trunkfishes by simulating a ray, and digging a pit. Many fishes will be attracted to the sand plume you create, hoping to find themselves a snack.

Space doesn't permit a full description of the sand flats, but we hope that you won't simply pass over them on the way to the coral. As long as you're burning air and time, why not have a good look around? After all, people travel thousands of miles to visit the desert.

The conch's eye at the end of a stalk provides vision while the animal is protected by its shell. (Photo: G. Lewbel.)

You will have to be very alert to spot animals such as this crab, which is colored like the sand and is often buried with only its back and eye stalks visible. (Photo: L. Martin.)

3

Marine Life

Cozumel has the usual suite of Caribbean reef fish, invertebrates, and plants. Although space does not permit a detailed listing of species, a few of the animals likely to be seen are described in this section. Divers will notice a definite zonation of groups of species that change with increasing depth and distance from shore. The zonation reflects decreasing levels of light and wave exposure with increasing depth, and increasing current velocities offshore. The zonation is most obvious among such reef-forming invertebrates as corals and sponges, but many fish are closely associated with the reef-builders and so show zonation themselves.

Corals

Very close to shore, perhaps the most prominent species is the elkhorn coral. It forms huge colonies that shelter long-spined sea urchins during the daytime. At night, the urchins move away from their shelters and graze on plants on the surrounding bottom. The largest gorgonians, or sea fans and sea whips, are near shore too. Divers are more likely to encounter fire coral in shallow water, growing on gorgonian skeletons, dead coral, or other surfaces.

Farther from shore, most of the reefs are dominated by the mountainous star coral and the cavernous star coral. In shallow water, these tend to grow as large mounds. As you probably know, corals are animals, but they have internal plants *(zooxanthellae)* which produce food and oxygen that are used by their hosts. The zooxanthellae need light to exist, and many species of corals change their growth forms depending on where they live in order to capture as much light as possible for their zooxanthellae. As a result, in deeper water (where there is not as much light) species such as the star corals tend to form sheets or plates that act like natural

◀ *A feathery basket star opens up at night. Many underwater creatures are visible or best seen only at night. (Photo: L. Martin.)*

solar collectors. The large buttresses, such as those on Palancar Reef, are built mainly by star corals, and the various growth forms can be seen at different depths. Species can always be recognized by the shape of the individual polyps, whatever the shape of the entire colony. The massive corals, such as the giant brain coral, are found over a wide depth range but are often larger in deeper water.

Other corals, such as the sheet or plate corals, specialize in living in low-light situations (crevices, overhangs, or deep water). These corals can become very large, thin, and fragile at depths where they are not likely to be broken by waves.

Anemones and Sponges

The common clubbed anemone frequently is seen with fluorescent tentacle tips. These tentacles bear the stinging cells with which this animal captures tiny crustaceans and other prey. Different colored tentacles do not indicate different species but rather color phases of the same species.

There are sponges wherever coral is found in Cozumel, and large sponges can be seen on nearly every dive. Look for the brittle stars in the purple vase sponges. Bristle worms (also called fire worms) are common everywhere, but can be seen breeding on purple vase sponges at night during the late fall. Many sponges look brown by daylight but are orange or blood-red by night or in strobe-lit photographs. The barrel sponges on the dropoffs have grown into funnel shapes under the influence of the usual south-to-north current. Their open cavities face north so that more stagnant water (carrying wastes from the sponge) is extracted from the funnel by passing current, and water with food and oxygen surrounds the outer filtering surface of the sponge.

Fishes

Fishes on Cozumel are extremely diverse, and most of the abundant reef species in the Caribbean can be seen at one time or another by divers on Cozumel. A few common nearshore species include yellow stingrays, barracudas, black groupers (handfed and tamed by divers on Palancar and Santa Rosa reefs), moray eels, angelfishes, butterfly fishes, wrasses, barjacks, grunts, snappers, and triggerfish. Chubs and yellow and black barred sergeant-majors will surround you, begging for food. Damselfishes will nip at you on every reef, and various parrotfishes can be seen and heard breaking coral with their jaws. Bigeye, glasseye snappers, and glassy sweepers are often seen hiding in shaded crevices in the daytime. Most photographers will want to search under coral heads at the edge of

When diving in Cozumel's waters, you are diving in a national preserve. The Mexican government considers illegal collecting and spearfishing a serious offense. (Photo: L. Martin.)

sandy patches for the elusive, splendid toadfish, a magnificent species in a family of fishes otherwise not known for their beauty. The splendid toadfish is believed to be common only in the vicinity of Cozumel Island. While looking under ledges for toadfish, you may find large spiny lobsters and crabs but note the following section if you're tempted to take dinner.

Spearfishing and Hunting Underwater

Most of the island's diveable reefs lie within a Mexican national preserve. Collection of any animals (including shells with living inhabitants) or plants within the preserve is strictly forbidden. Outside of the preserve, sport fishing is allowed if you have a Mexican fishing license.

The Mexican game fishing regulations are fairly complex, and include bag and seasonal restrictions on many species. Scuba could be used for collecting fish and lobsters as of this printing. Fishing licenses can be requested from the Oficina de Pesca (Fish Office) in San Miguel on Cozumel Island (ask a taxi driver where it is). Prices for the licenses currently are changing but have been nominal in the past for short trips. Take the time to ask for a copy of the most recent regulations, though, and ask specifically about diving requirements. Be careful! The Mexican government takes illegal collecting very seriously, and a large fine including the gear used for the collection (i.e., all of your diving equipment and the boat!) would not be out of the ordinary. Spear guns are usually seized by customs upon entry to Cozumel, just in case you might be tempted to stray.

4

Safety

This section discusses common hazards, including dangerous marine animals, and emergency procedures in case of a diving accident. We do not discuss the diagnosis or treatment of serious medical problems; refer to your first aid manual or emergency diving accident manual for that information.

We also suggest some ways to contact qualified medical personnel as rapidly as possible, based partly on responses to our own inquiries for this volume and partly on information supplied by other sources. The telephone numbers and addresses given in this edition were current to the best of the authors' knowledge in late 1990, but the authors assume no responsibility for assuring that phone numbers or contact information are correct. Emergency contact information can change unpredictably when personnel and facilities move, get new telephone numbers, and so on. Readers are advised to check on emergency contact information during or just before the time of their dive trip.

Diving Accidents

In case of a diving accident such as a lung overpressure injury (e.g., air embolism, pneumothorax, mediastinal emphysema) or decompression sickness ("bends"), prompt recompression treatment in a chamber may be essential to prevent permanent injury or death.

Local Facilities: As of late 1990, there are two recompression chambers on Cozumel Island. The older facility is at the hospital *(Centro de Salud),* a few blocks from the water on Calle 11 Sur. Calle 11 Sur intersects Avenida Rafael Melgar (the street along the waterfront) near the Hotel Barracuda, toward the southern side of town. The hospital's phone number is 2-01-40.

The hospital will recompress you if the other chamber is occupied, or if you prefer to go the low-budget route. Because the hospital is government funded, the cost of a chamber treatment may be as low as several

Boat traffic is a serious hazard in Cozumel. Be especially alert for boat noise, look around during ascents when near the surface, and be proficient at buoyancy control during ascents and while performing safety stops. (Photo: L. Martin.)

hundred dollars. However, the hospital chamber is used mainly for non-diving-related hyperbaric oxygen treatments and for injured Mexican nationals, rather than for tourists. If you look as if you can afford the high-priced spread, you will probably find yourself shunted to the Servicios chamber.

This may be to your advantage. In the past, reports on the hospital's chamber have been mixed, and, frankly, recompression therapy seems like a bad place to try to save a buck or two. For a long time, oxygen had to be brought over to Cozumel from the mainland, and was not always available at the chamber. At present, oxygen cylinders can be filled on the island, which has greatly improved the hospital's chamber operations. Nonetheless, most injured tourists are being treated by Servicios at this time.

The Servicios chamber is geared specifically for diving tourists. It is operated as a private venture by Servicios de Seguridad Sub-Acuatica. It is located on Calle 5 Sur, around the corner from Aqua Safari and about one block from the water, next to Discover Diving. Servicios staff can be telephoned at 2-18-48.

The Red Cross *(Cruz Roja)* can provide an ambulance if contacted by phone (2-10-58) or by VHF radio on Channel 16. Servicios can set up ambulance transportation and simultaneously prepare for your arrival at the chamber. Servicios also can assist you in reaching other physicians, e.g. for non-diving problems.

It should be emphasized that the chamber situation may be completely different by the time you arrive on Cozumel. Emergency numbers change, and chambers wax and wane depending upon their funding and staff. We strongly recommend that you ask your booking agent to provide you with reliable emergency information at the time that you make your reservations. Furthermore, we suggest that you check this information with DAN (see below), given the state of flux in Mexico. Upon arrival, we also suggest you ask your dive operator how to cope with a diving emergency or other accident. Don't accept a vague answer. You should interpret the absence of a workable accident management plan as a lack of both professionalism and concern for your welfare.

If this all sounds a little paranoid, be warned that it isn't. Some of those old horror stories about botched evacuations and bungled recompression treatments in Cozumel are true. It's a long way back to the States if you have a medical problem. The trip may involve extensive bureaucratic juggling, expense, and delays. Keep an eye on your gauges, make slow ascents and safety stops, and here — more than many other places — don't push your luck.

DAN: Whether or not you choose to accept local treatment, our recommendation is that you contact the Divers Alert Network (DAN) in the United States immediately in case of a diving injury. DAN, a membership association of individuals and organizations sharing a common interest in diving safety, operates a **24-hour national hotline, (919) 684-8111** (collect calls are accepted in an emergency). DAN does not directly provide medical care; however, they do provide advice on first aid, evacuation, and hyperbaric treatment of diving-related injuries. For further information, contact DAN, Duke University Medical Center, Box 3823, Durham, NC 27710.

Divers should contact DAN as soon as a diving emergency is suspected. All divers should have comprehensive medical insurance and check to make sure that hyperbaric treatment and air ambulance services are covered internationally.

Air Ambulance Service: If you elect to leave Cozumel for treatment, you are probably going to need a chartered flight with medical equipment and personnel on board, in an aircraft capable of pressurization at the equivalent of sea-level (1 atmosphere). Several air ambulance companies in the United States can provide this service, but flying in Mexico requires some red tape that is best taken care of in advance. Under ideal circumstances you will probably wait at least four hours after you request an aircraft before it lands in Cozumel.

You should be aware that the cost of an evacuation flight will be high and that payment will be expected either in Mexico or promptly after arrival in the States. You will most likely be asked to provide proof of financial responsibility in the form of cash, check, or credit cards, or to furnish names and phone numbers of friends or relatives in the States who will guarantee the cost of the flight. Brace yourself for a bill that may run $8,000 (U.S.) or more, depending on how fast an aircraft you need (this may be your chance to ride in a Lear Jet), what medical equipment and personnel need to be on board, its point of origin, and its destination.

Emergency Contacts — Recheck upon arrival!
Subject to change.

Recompression Chambers (Cozumel):
 Hospital: Tel. 2-01-40
 Servicios: Tel. 2-18-48

Divers Alert Network (DAN): Tel. (919) 684-8111
 (for assistance in dealing with Cozumel recompression chambers
 or for finding a chamber in the U.S.)

Air ambulance services (to U.S. recompression chambers) Life
 Flight (Houston, TX): Tel. (800) 231-4357 (U.S.);
 (800) 392-4357 (TX)
 (713) 797-4357

Common Hazardous Marine Animals

Sea Urchins: The most common hazardous animal divers will encounter around Cozumel is the long-spined sea urchin. This urchin has spines that are capable of penetrating wetsuits, booties, and gloves like a knife through butter. Injuries are nearly always immediately painful, and sometimes infect. Urchins are found at every diving depth, although they are more common in shallow water near shore, especially under coral heads. At night the urchins come out of their hiding places and are even easier to bump into. Minor injuries can be dealt with by extracting the spines (easier said than done!) and treating the wound with antibiotic cream. Make sure your tetanus immunization is current; serious punctures will require a doctor's attention. The easiest way to find a doctor is to go to the hospital (see previous section), or to ask any hotel desk to call one for you.

Fire Coral: Fire coral is most common in shallow water, but can grow as an encrusting form on dead gorgonians or coral at any depth. Contact with fire coral causes a burning feeling which usually goes away in a minute or two. In some individuals, contact results in red welts. Cortisone cream can reduce the inflammation. Coral cuts and scrapes also can irritate and frequently infect. We've treated minor coral scratches successfully with antibiotic cream, but serious cuts should be handled by a doctor, especially if broken bits of coral are embedded in the wound.

Bristle or Fire Worms: Bristle worms, also called fire worms, can be found on most reefs with a little searching. If you touch one with bare skin it will embed tiny, stinging bristles in your skin and cause a burning sensation that may be followed by the development of a red spot or welt. The sensation is similar to touching fire coral or massaging one of those fuzzy, soft-looking cactuses on land. The bristles will eventually work their way out of your skin in a couple of days. You can try to scrape them off with the edge of a sharp knife. Cortisone cream helps reduce local inflammation.

Sponges: Sponges also have fine spicules, and some species (so-called fire sponges) have a chemical irritant that is immediately painful. Although bright red color is sometimes a clue to the bad ones, it's not completely reliable. We have been stung by various innocuous-looking sponges. If you get spicules in your skin, try scraping them off with the edge of a sharp knife. We've also tried pouring mild vinegar solutions and mild ammonia solutions on the parts that hurt; sometimes they work, sometimes they don't. The stinging sensation usually goes away within a day, and cortisone cream helps.

A bristle worm makes its way across a giant brain coral colony. (Photo: G. Lewbel.)

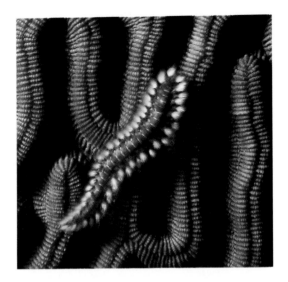

A yellow stingray cruises the sand flats. (Photo: L. Martin.)

Rays: Sand flats around Cozumel are inhabited by two species of sting rays, the southern sting ray (very large, wary, and difficult to approach), and the yellow sting ray (small, well-camouflaged, and easy to approach). Sting rays are not especially aggressive, but they don't take kindly to being sat on, patted, or stepped on. If you leave them alone, they'll leave you alone. If you insist on a 1:1 macro shot of a sting ray nostril you will probably be stung by the long, barbed stinger at the base of the tail. Wounds are always extremely painful, are often deep and infective, and can cause serious symptoms including anaphylactic shock. If you get stung, head for the hospital and ask a doctor to take care of the wound.

Moray Eels: Moray eels are dangerous only if harassed. There are lots of morays under coral heads and in crevices. In recent years, divers at other islands have hand-fed morays, but this practice has not yet become widespread on Cozumel. One of the authors who was involved in a scientific fish-tagging experiment can attest personally to the biting ability of green morays (number of needle-like teeth, penetration depth, number of stitches required, etc.). If you watch where you stick your hands, however, you will not have to test Mexican morays' dispositions. Bites are sometimes infective and very painful and call for a doctor's attention.

Scorpionfish: Scorpionfish are well-camouflaged, small fish (usually less than a foot long) that have poisonous spines hidden among their fins. They are often difficult to spot, since they typically sit quietly on the bottom looking more like plant-covered rocks than fish. As with sting rays, watch where you put your hands and knees and you're not likely to meet one the hard way. If you get stung, severe allergic reactions are quite possible and great pain and infection are virtually certain, so head for the hospital and see a doctor.

Sharks: We are not aware of any reported shark attacks at Cozumel. Sharks are very uncommon at most of the reefs around Cozumel but several small blacktips recently have taken up residence near Santa Rosa Reef. Sharks are also seen more often at Maracaibo Reef than other sites, and nurse sharks are sometimes spotted sleeping under ledges at Yocab and San Juan reefs. Please don't tug on nurse sharks' tails while they are asleep, by the way, even though it's tempting. They wake up grumpy and have bitten a number of divers in other locations. Any shark injury obviously calls for immediate medical attention.

◀ *A well-camouflaged spotted scorpionfish rests almost motionless on a rocky surface. These creatures have poisonous spines that can inflict extremely painful and often danger- ous wounds. Watch where you place your hands and feet; these are difficult fish to spot. If you are stung, see a doctor at once. (Photo: G. Lewbel.)*

Barracuda: Barracudas are included in this section only because of their undeserved reputation for ferocity. There are a few unconfirmed reports of attacks on swimmers in dirty water in other locations, but you'll have nothing to worry about on Cozumel. You'll be lucky to get one close enough for a good photograph. They're rather timid about coming closer than a few yards. At night, though, you can sometimes get within touching distance of a sleeping barracuda.

Barracudas are often difficult for divers to approach. The best tactic for getting a close look is to hold still and wait for them to investigate you. (Photo: G. Lewbel.)

Appendix 1: Further Reading

The most accessible information on Cozumel Island (other than this guide) can be found in articles in *Ocean Realm* and *Skin Diver* magazines or in *In Depth*. If you don't subscribe to one of these publications you can probably find at least one of them in your local library, and most dive shops that run trips to Cozumel maintain a file of clippings. However, magazine articles and books go out of date, needless to say. It's hard to find published articles that are current on hotels, dive operators, and other topside facilities. On Cozumel, personnel and facilities change very rapidly compared to other Caribbean Islands. By the time material is published, it may already contain inaccuracies even though it was correct at the time it was written.

The most consistently reliable sources about Cozumel's hotels, dive operators, and other topside facilities are dive travel specialists and dive shop owners who have been there recently. The dive travel industry must keep up with the local scene, since reservations and bookings have to be correct. A call or visit to someone who just spent a week on the island will provide you with more useful information than via almost any other means.

To learn more about the fish and corals you will see while diving around Cozumel, we recommend that you purchase a copy of Idaz and Jerry Greenberg's book, *Guide to Corals and Fishes of Florida, the Bahamas, and the Caribbean,* published by Seahawk Press, 6840 SW 92nd Street, Miami, Florida 33156. The book, available from most dive shops in the States as well as on the island, is available in a waterproof version you can take underwater, as well as a topside version. For more detail, we suggest Patrick Colin's book, *Caribbean Reef Invertebrates and Plants,* from TFH Publications, Inc., P.O. Box 27, Neptune City, New Jersey 07753.

On arrival, you should also obtain three very helpful publications: *The Blue Guide* (free at almost every hotel and dive store); and the Blue Map and the Brown Map (a couple of dollars each, same places). The *Blue Guide* is a tourist-oriented compendium of local phone numbers, dollars-to-pesos conversion tables, coupons, ads, clothing size charts, etc. The Brown Map shows roads, ruins, parks, beaches, recompression chambers, hospital locations, etc. The Blue Map ("Chart of the Reefs . . .") shows many of the dive sites in this book.

Appendix 2: Dive Shops

This list is included as a service to the reader. The publisher has made every effort to make this list complete at the time the book was printed. This list does not constitute an endorsement of these operators and dive shops. If operators/owners wish to be included in future reprints/editions, please contact Pisces Books, P.O. Box 2608, Houston, Texas 77252-2608.

Aqua Safari
P.O. Box 41
Cozumel, Quintana Roo 77600
México
Phone: (987) 201-01
FAX: (987) 206-61

Aqua Sports Maya
P.O. Box 317
Cozumel, Quintana Roo
México
FAX: (987) 223-48

Blue Angel Scuba School
P.O. Box 280
Cozumel, Quintana Roo 77600
México
Phone: (987) 216-31
FAX: (987) 209-13

Blue Bubble Divers
P.O. Box 334
Isla Cozumel, Q.R. 77600
México
Phone/FAX: (987) 218-65

Caribbean Divers
P.O. Box 191
Cozumel, Quintana Roo 77600
México
Phone: (987) 210-80
FAX: (987) 214-26

Club Cozumel Caribe
P.O. Box 43
Cozumel, Quintana Roo 77600
México
Phone: (987) 200-21
FAX: (987) 202-88

Del Mar Aquatics
P.O. Box 129
Cozumel, Quintana Roo 77600
México
Phone: (987) 219-44
FAX: (987) 218-33

Dive House
P.O. Box 246
Isla Cozumel, Q.R. 77600
México
Phone: (987) 219-53
FAX: (987) 230-68

Dive Paradise
P.O. Box 222
Isla Cozumel, Q.R. 77600
México
Phone: (987) 210-07
FAX: (987) 210-61

El Clavado Dive Shop
Mr. Edwin Garcia
P.O. Box 38
Cozumel, Quintana Roo 77600
Phone/Fax: (987) 230-58
(Chankanab only)

Fantasia Divers
25 Ave. Entre A. Rosado Y3 Sur
Cozumel, Quintana Roo 77600
México
FAX: (987) 212-10

Ramón Zapata Divers
Parque Chankanab
Cozumel, Quintana Roo 77600
México
Phone: (987) 217-82

Scuba Shack
P.O. Box 192
Isla Cozumel QR 77600
México
Phone/FAX: (987) 201-45

Scuba Tours
P.O. Box 307
Isla Cozumel, Q.R. 77600
México
Phone: (987) 236-56
FAX: (987) 230-46

Victor Brito
P.O. Box 349
Cozumel, Quintana Roo 77600
México
Phone/FAX: (987) 232-23

Wild Cat Divers
Calle 2 Nte. #99
Cozumel, Quintana Roo 77600
México
Phone/FAX: (987) 210-28

Yucab Reef
P.O. Box 316
Cozumel, Quintana Roo 77600
México
FAX: (987) 218-42

Index

A quick climb up the ladder ends another great day of diving in Cozumel. (Photo: L. Martin.)